The Word System

by
Happy Caldwell

HARRISON HOUSE
Tulsa, Oklahoma

Unless otherwise indicated,
all Scripture quotations are from
the *King James Version* of the Bible.

ISBN 0-89274-176-7
Copyright © 1981 by Happy Caldwell
Agape Ministries, Inc.
P. O. Box 5232
Little Rock, AR 72215

Published by Harrison House, Inc.
P. O. Box 35035
Tulsa, OK 74135

Printed in the United States of America
All Rights Reserved

Contents

Introduction
1	The Beginning	7
2	Man's Need for God's System	13
3	The Law of Choice	23
4	"Poor Old Job"	35
5	Jesus, The Last Adam	43
6	Operating the Word System	49

Introduction

We live in a world filled with words.

Have you ever stopped to think what it would be like without them?

Words are communication. They are used to express feelings, desires, love, compassion, even hate.

Without words, there would be no verbal expression. We would live in a world without intelligent human sound, and the human race would be reduced to a much lower state of expression.

With this in mind, have you ever wondered why words are the prime means of communication? Words are vital to us because we are made in the image of God, and God operated under a word system.

Maybe you have wondered why there has been such an increase in teaching about the words we speak, commonly called "the confession teaching." There is good reason for this kind of teaching in the Church today.

Some Christians are verbally destroying themselves — literally killing themselves — with their own words. Others, however, are turning their captivity by changing their words. They have become conquerors instead of failures, prosperous instead of in poverty.

Whatever your circumstances in life, you can change them if you will learn God's system of operation: *The Word System.*

1

The Beginning

Several years ago, while on the Gulf Coast of Florida, I was taking time to rest and meditate on the Word of God. One evening as I was sitting on the beach, watching the waves roll in, the Holy Spirit began to speak to me about God's system of operation.

He showed me God's word system.

In the beginning God created the heaven and the earth.

And the earth was without form, and void; and darkness was upon the face of the deep. And the Spirit of God moved upon the face of the waters.

And God said . . . .

Genesis 1:1-3

This is how God began His system: He spoke words. *And God said, Let there be light: and there was light* (v. 3). The words, *God said . . .* , appear eight more times in the first chapter of Genesis. Each time He spoke, something was created, formed, or made.

Many times people have the wrong idea or concept of God. They see Him as an old man, floating around on a bunch of clouds; but the Bible says God is love.

God is a personal being, and you were made in His image.

I remember a story about a little boy who came home from vacation Bible school. When his father asked him what he had learned, the boy handed him a picture he had drawn. The picture was of a red Cadillac convertible. In the front seat was an old man with long gray whiskers. In the back seat was a man and woman.

The father asked, "What is this?"

The boy answered proudly, "That's God driving Adam and Eve out of the Garden!" (Well, at least he had God driving a red Cadillac. Some folks would put Him in a Model T, just barely making it around!)

God made man in His own image:

God said, Let us make man in our image, after our likeness: and let them have dominion over the fish of the sea, and over the fowl of the air, and over the cattle, and over all the earth, and over every creeping thing that creepeth upon the earth.

So God created man in his own image, in the image of God created he him; male and female created he them.
Genesis 1:26,27

What is "the image of God"? If we are created in His image, we need to know what that image is. The Bible says God is a Spirit, and those that worship Him must worship Him in spirit and in truth. (John 4:23.) But God is much more than a Spirit. He had substance. He wanted us to see Him and know Him, so He sent a representation of Himself, Jesus Christ.

Jesus represented God's substance. Hebrews 1:1-3 says:

God, who at sundry times and in divers manners spake in time past unto the fathers by the prophets,

Hath in these last days spoken unto us by his Son, whom he hath appointed heir of all things, by whom also he made the worlds.

Who being the brightness of his glory, and the express image of his person . . . .

This is referring to Jesus. Literally, it is rendered "the representation of the substance of God." Jesus was the express image of God. He was God in the flesh.

In Genesis 1:26, God said, *Let us make man in our image.* What do the words "us" and "our" refer to? They refer to the person and personality of God: God the Father, God the Son, and God the Holy Spirit.

We as human beings are made in this same image. We are triune beings just like God: spirit, soul, and body.

The real you is a spirit; and you have a soul (your will, intellect, emotions, desires, mind), and you live in a body.

Your physical body is not the real you. It is just a tabernacle or tent, something for you to move around in. When the body dies, the spirit man lives on. It will go to one of two places: to be with God or to be with the devil.

The man on the street may say, "Oh, there's no life after death; it's just over."

Well, I have news for him: He has been told a lie, and he will find out the truth one of these days.

As I was praying one day, I kept saying the same words over and over: "God, make me like Jesus. I want to be like Jesus. Make me like Jesus." The desire of my heart was to operate my life with all the love, compassion, and faith that Jesus operated in while He lived on earth; so I just kept saying, "Make me like Jesus."

Suddenly, God said, "Son, you're asking Me to do something I've already done."

God had already made me like Jesus. I was made in His image, and Jesus was His image. He said, "If you really want to get scriptural about it, I made Jesus like you."

The Word became flesh. Philippians 2:7 says, *And* (Jesus) *took upon him the form of a servant, and was made in the likeness of men.*

Do you know who you are?

You are *not* an old unworthy worm in the dust, just barely making it along.

You may say, "I'm just a sinner, saved by grace." Well, I am not saying that you cannot sin; I am saying you are not a sin creature. If you have been born again, you no longer have a sin nature.

Yes, you *were* a sinner — unworthy, no-good, ugly; but when you were saved, you crossed over from sin to righteousness. You came out of the darkness, and now you are walking in the light. You are now the righteousness of God.

You have been made in the image and likeness of God for a purpose: God made man in His own image so he could act like God.

"Brother Happy, do you mean I'm supposed to act like God?"

Yes, that's right. This is what is wrong with the Church today. They have been acting like heathens when they should have been acting like God.

You may say, "I wouldn't dare act like God!"

Well, you had better because that is what a Christian is supposed to do. Being a Christian is to be a "little Christ," a follower (imitator) of God. (Eph. 5:1.)

2

Man's Need for God's System

Your understanding of the word system will make a great difference in your life. By becoming aware of how God's system operates, you can oppose the devil in any way he might come against you. He will never be able to stop you from getting your job done when you know how God operates.

God established a system that used words for a reason. God made man in His own image so man could operate the system the same way God did.

Again, Genesis 1:26 says that man was to have dominion over the fish of the sea, the fowl of the air, the cattle, over all the earth, and over every creeping thing that crawled on the earth.

How was man going to have this dominion over the creation of God? With words!

God made this earth for you and me. He did not make it for Himself, nor did He make it for the devil. He made it for His man. He intended for man to subdue the earth and take dominion over everything in it.

I recall an incident some time ago that illustrates what I am talking about.

Charles Capps and I were on a fishing trip, and I had just hooked a large bass on a "Lucky 13" lure. (I call it a "Blessed 13.") When I pulled the bass to the side of the boat, my line broke. I lost the fish *and* my "Blessed 13"!

I said, "Doesn't that beat all! I lost the fish and my best fishing lure."

Charles said, "Why don't you tell that fish to jump up out of the water and spit the bait back to you? After all, you have authority over the fish in this lake according to Philippians 2:10."

I thought to myself, "Do I dare say that? Yes, I do!"

So I yelled, "Fish that stole my lure, you jump up out of the water and spit my bait back to me!"

About two or three minutes later, that fish jumped out of the water, just like he was posing for a sports magazine, and spit out that bait, right in front of my face! (We had drifted a distance from where I had lost the fish, so he had to swim hard to find us again!)

If you have trouble believing fish stories, let me give you a testimony that came as a result of this:

After I shared my story in a meeting in Virginia, a young man was able to use

God's word system in his own life when a bird flew into his house. He and his family tried to catch it, but with no success.

Then he remembered the word system and the example I had used; so he told his family to stand still and he would speak to the bird. He said, "Bird, fly up and light on my finger," and the bird did just as he commanded! He then opened the patio door and the bird flew out.

God showed Adam how to operate the word system. In the Garden, they had fellowship together constantly. They talked with one another and walked together.

Have you ever had God tell you, "Get up; let's go for a walk"? I have had Him do that to me quite frequently.

"Brother Happy, you mean God talks to you like that?"

Yes, and He will talk to you, too, if you will just listen. But you can't listen when the television is going full blast!

In Genesis 2:18,19, you can see Adam begin to operate the word system:

The Lord God said, It is not good that the man should be alone; I will make him an help meet for him.

And out of the ground the Lord God formed every beast of the field, and every fowl of the air; and brought them unto Adam to see what he would call them: and whatsoever Adam called every living creature, that was the name thereof.

This is the first record we have of Adam operating the word system: He named the creatures on earth.

Picture in your mind Adam naming every beast of the field and every fowl of the air. He was already discovering how to use God's system — speaking words of faith and power. Through his mouth, Adam was speaking creative words, calling every creature by name — the name it would have forever.

You see, God is a faith God. Hebrews 11:3 says, *Through faith we understand that the worlds were framed by the word of God.* He had to use His faith to get everything started in the first place and He expects no more or less of us than He expects of Himself.

Adam gave names to all cattle, and to the fowl of the air, and to every beast of the field; but for Adam there was not found an help meet for him.

And the Lord God caused a deep sleep to fall upon Adam, and he slept: and he took one of his ribs, and closed up the flesh instead thereof;

And the rib, which the Lord God had taken from man, made he a woman, and brought her unto the man.

Genesis 2:20-22

Adam has operated the word system by naming all the beasts on earth. Then God makes a woman as a "help meet" for Adam and brings her to him. He continues the word system by speaking words of power and creative authority over her. He prophesies over her; and when he does, he sounds just like God — he even uses the same language.

And Adam Said . . .

Notice what he says in Genesis 2:23,24:

This is now bone of my bones, and flesh of my flesh: she shall be called Woman, because she was taken out of Man. Therefore shall a man leave his father and his mother, and shall cleave unto his wife: and they shall be one flesh.

Adam prophesied the ordination of marriage. The words he spoke over the institution of marriage have remained to this day. Jesus referred to it in the first two Gospels, and Paul spoke of it in the Epistles.

Adam operated God's word system, and he did it as a man.

You and I today are made in the same image and likeness of God. When we are redeemed from the old sin nature, we take upon ourselves the righteous nature of God. We are joint-heirs with Jesus and He was the last Adam:

The first man Adam was made a living soul; the last Adam was made a quickening spirit (1 Cor. 15:45).

God made us in His image, and He gave us the ability and authority to use His system of words.

This makes clear the recent emphasis on the confession teaching. It no longer remains just a "mouth trip," but a system established by God. It is the way we are to operate here on earth.

We are to speak the words of God with our mouths as they come up from our hearts. This is what Jesus meant when He said, *Out of the abundance of the heart the mouth speaketh* (Matt. 12:34).

In the parable of the sower from Mark, chapter 4, Jesus explained how the Word goes into the heart of man, likening it to a seed going into the earth. The seed is the Word of God and the earth is the heart of man.

The seed of God's Word must be sown into your heart, and your heart was designed by God to produce what is sown there. This is why Jesus said to watch what you hear: What goes into the ears will go down into the heart.

The words you speak are what your heart will believe, and they can work for you or against you.

You can say, "I don't feel good; I feel like I'm getting the flu," and you probably will.

Or, you can say, "Praise God, I'm healed by the stripes of Jesus. I don't care what I see, taste, smell, hear, or feel. I'm healed." And you will be!

The importance of understanding the word system is to speak the words of God.

While I was on that beach in Florida, meditating on these things, I said, "God, do You mean that if I operated this system completely and totally, 100%, I could call those things that are not as though they were, and I could say to those waves breaking on the sand, 'Waves, stop!' and they would stop?"

He said, "Yes, they would; but the secret is in John 15:7. If you abide in Me and My words abide in you, *then* you can ask what you will. There is only one man who has operated this system 100%, and that was Jesus. It takes discipline."

There are some men who are approaching that 100% mark, but they aren't there yet.

I said, "Lord, I want to be one of those men!"

He said, "It's up to you. You can do it if you will discipline yourself to abide in My Word and allow My Word to abide in you."

When I told God I wanted to operate His system, He said, "Then don't speak anything but the Word of God."

I thought, "Oh, God, I'd be a weirdo. People would look at me like I was nutty."

He said, "Yes, they sure would, but I have already said you were a peculiar person, so what do you care what they think?"

As I meditated on what He had said, I formed a mental image of a man who spoke nothing but the Word of God. I saw him going to a neighbor's house for fellowship one evening. When the door opened, they grabbed his hand and said, "Well, how are you feeling today?"

He answered, "According to 1 Peter 2:24, I'm healed by the stripes of Jesus."

They said, "We've had a lot of rain lately; I don't know what we're going to do about the weather."

He responds, "According to Genesis 8:22, as long as the earth remains, seedtime and harvest shall not cease."

He would be a funny fellow talking nothing but the Word of God, but he could walk in the word system.

3

The Law of Choice

Man was made in the image of God. He was placed in dominion over the earth and was given the ability to choose right and wrong. The law of choice was instituted.

In Genesis 2:15-17, we can see the choice God gave to Adam.

The Lord God took the man, and put him into the garden of Eden to dress it and to keep it.

And the Lord God commanded the man, saying, Of every tree of the garden thou mayest freely eat:

But of the tree of the knowledge of good and evil, thou shalt not eat of it: for in the day that thou eatest thereof thou shalt surely die.

Notice, the tree was not "of good and evil," nor were there two trees — one good and one evil. It was "the tree of the *knowledge* of good and evil." Both good and evil existed; but Adam did not know evil, he only knew good. To be legal, God had to give man a choice, so Adam had a choice from the very beginning.

I want to show you the law of choice. The word system works together with the law of choice.

How art thou fallen from heaven, O Lucifer, son of the morning! how art thou cut down to the ground, which didst weaken the nations!

For thou hast said in thine heart, I will ascend into heaven, I will exalt my throne above the stars of God: I will sit also upon the mount of the congregation, in the sides of the north: I will ascend above the heights of the clouds; I will be like the most High . . .

They that see thee shall narrowly look upon thee, and consider thee, saying, Is this the man that made the earth to tremble, that did shake kingdoms . . .? (Is. 14:12-14,16).

In Ezekiel 28 we see God exposing an earthly king and also an unseen ruler. The scripture applies to both a visible person and an invisible one. (This is called the law of double reference.)

Moreover the word of the Lord came unto me, saying, Son of man, take up a lamentation upon the king of Tyrus, and say unto him, Thus saith the Lord God; Thou sealest up the sum, full of wisdom, and perfect in beauty.

(He begins to talk about Satan:) *Thou hast been in Eden the garden of God;*

every precious stone was thy covering, the sardius, topaz, and the diamond, the beryl, the onyx, and the jasper, the sapphire, the emerald, and the carbuncle, and gold: the workmanship of thy tabrets and of thy pipes was prepared in thee in the day that thou was created.

Thou art the anointed cherub that covereth; and I have set thee so: thou wast upon the holy mountain of God; thou hast walked up and down in the midst of the stones of fire. Thou wast perfect in thy ways from the day that thou wast created, till iniquity was found in thee.

By the multitude of thy merchandise they have filled the midst of thee with violence, and thou hast sinned: therefore I will cast thee as profane out of the mountain of God: and I will destroy thee, O covering cherub, from the midst of the stones of fire.

(Here is how Satan sinned:) *Thine heart was lifted up because of thy beauty, thou hast corrupted thy wisdom by reason of thy brightness: I will cast thee to the ground, I will lay thee before kings, that they may behold thee.*

Thou hast defiled thy sanctuaries by the multitude of thine iniquities, by the iniquity of thy traffick; therefore will I bring forth a fire from the midst of thee, it shall devour thee, and I will bring thee to ashes upon the earth in the sight of all them that behold thee.

In this passage, Lucifer (Satan) was reigning and ruling over the original creation as "son of the morning." He was a beautiful angel, a created being, who said, *I will exalt my throne above the stars of God* (Is. 14:13). He was in open rebellion. Where was he at this time? He was on earth, in Eden. (When it says he was in Eden, it is referring to a time before Adam was there.)

Lucifer tried to rebel and take over the throne of God, but he was defeated by God and cast down to the earth.

When I began to meditate on the law of choice in relation to the word system, I had to go back further than Adam on the earth. The tree of the knowledge of good and evil was there to give Adam a choice. But where did the knowledge of evil originate?

I said, "God, I've got to know. If you gave Adam a choice and told him not to eat of the tree of the knowledge of good and evil, then where did evil come from to begin with?"

I kept coming back to the fact that God was a perfect and good God, so He could not have created evil. (Though Isaiah 45:7 says that the Lord creates evil, the word "create" does not mean "to originate." It means "to allow the choice of evil.")

James says every good and perfect gift comes from the Father above. (James 1:17.) He says in verse 13, *Let no man say when he is tempted, I am tempted of God: for God cannot be tempted with evil, neither tempteth he any man* (with evil).

God was not the author of evil, so where did evil come from?

Satan sinned against God, and evil was the result of sin. However, the Bible says that Lucifer was perfect in his ways (Ezek. 28:15), and that is where I could not quite put it together. If he was perfect, how could he sin?

I kept coming back to the law of choice. If Satan sinned of his own free will, then he must have chosen to do so. He must have been created with a free will to choose between righteousness and iniquity.

Where was I going to find in the Scriptures that Satan had a free will of choice? Did he truly have a choice? I again read Isaiah 14 and Ezekiel 28.

What finally dawned on me was that he did have a choice because he made one! If he did not have a choice, how could he have made one? If he had no opportunity to choose between good and evil, how could he have done it? Lucifer had a choice. Everything God created had a choice!

The law of choice undoubtedly began with God, and He even made the choice available to Lucifer.

There is a law in physics that says, "For every action, there is an equal and opposite reaction." Satan put this law into operation against himself. God was total perfection: total good, total righteousness. Satan, by his own free will, said, "I am going to depart from the good and the righteous," and when he did, he set in motion the exact opposite. He sinned, and sin brought forth evil.

Now let's go back to Adam in the Garden. Because God is a just and legal God, He had to give Adam that same choice of good and evil: *But of the tree of the knowledge of good and evil, thou shalt not eat of it: for in the day that thou eatest thereof thou shalt surely die* (Gen. 2:17). If God had not given Adam the choice, as He had every other being, Satan could have demanded justice.

After reading the account in Genesis 3:1-6, we know that the devil beguiled Eve through the serpent. Adam and Eve sinned by doing what God told them not to do: eat of the tree of the knowledge of good and evil. They came to know good and evil.

Genesis 3:1 says, *Now the serpent was more subtil than any beast of the field which the Lord God had made. And he said unto the woman, Yea, hath God said, Ye shall not eat of every tree of the garden?* Notice the question. The devil comes to all of us with questions and tempting thoughts. With Satan, the battleground is in the realm of the mind.

If you will renew your mind with the Word of God and then speak it, the devil has no recourse against you; he will not be able to motivate you.

He will throw suggestions at you such as, "Did God *really* say by the stripes of Jesus you were healed? Did God *really* say you could have what you say? Did He *really* say He would supply all your needs?"

When he does, you will be able to speak the Word to the devil and defeat him.

You see, he always comes with a question as he did to Eve: *Yea, hath God said, Ye shall not eat of every tree of the garden?*

And the woman said unto the serpent, We may eat of the fruit of the trees of the garden: But of the fruit of the tree which is in the midst of the garden, God hath said, Ye shall not eat of it, neither shall ye touch it, lest ye die.

The serpent said unto the woman, Ye shall not surely die (Gen. 3:1-4).

What a lie! God said just the opposite.

The serpent continues: *For God doth know that in the day ye eat thereof, then your eyes shall be opened, and ye shall be as gods, knowing good and evil.*

When the woman saw that the tree was good for food, and that it was pleasant to the eyes, and a tree to be desired to make one wise, she took of the fruit thereof, and did eat, and gave also unto her husband with her; and he did eat.

Both Adam and Eve did what God told them not to do. They *chose* to eat of the tree. Why? It was appealing to the senses.

The tree was "good for food" (the lust of the flesh). It was "pleasant to the eyes" (the lust of the eyes). It was "desired to make one wise" (the pride of life).

Satan is the tempter, and he uses the same three temptations in every area of life. But Jesus came to earth as a man and conquered those same temptations, and He did it by using the word system. (Remember this; we will come back to it in a later chapter.)

I want you to see how the law of choice relates to the word system. Leviticus 5:4 says:

If a soul swear, pronouncing with his lips to do evil, or to do good, whatsoever it be that a man shall pronounce with an oath, and it be hid from him; when he knoweth of it, then he shall be guilty in one of these.

The word "guilty" means that he shall be punished or perish because of what he has said with his mouth. In other words, he will receive the results of the statement he made.

Let me give you an example: How many times have you stepped into your car to drive down the street and had something act up on your car? Every time it acts up, you say, "You sorry, no-good car! You always give me trouble." If you continue saying that, you will have what you say.

In Deuteronomy, chapter 30, God talks again to His people about the law of choice in relation to the word system. Keep in mind that God has already told the people the things that bring the blessings and the curse.

For this commandment which I command thee this day, it is not hidden from thee, neither is it far off.

It is not in heaven, that thou shouldest say, Who shall go up for us to heaven, and bring it unto us, that we may hear it, and do it?

Neither is it beyond the sea, that thou shouldest say, Who shall go over the sea for us, and bring it unto us, that we may hear it, and do it?

But the word (God's Word!) *is very nigh unto thee, in thy mouth, and in thy heart, that thou mayest do it.*

See, I have set before thee this day life and good, death and evil.

Deuteronomy 30:11-15

Notice the choice: You can have life or death, good or evil. It's up to you. Both the Law and the Word were set before the children of Israel. It was their choice what they would have. God said the Word is in your mouth: Whatever you say with your mouth is what you will have.

Now, look at verses 16-19:

In that I command thee this day to love the Lord thy God, to walk in his ways, and to keep his commandments and his statutes and his judgments, that thou mayest live and multiply: and the Lord thy God shall bless thee in the land whither thou goest to possess it.

But if thine heart turn away (that is what happened to Satan: his heart turned away), *so that thou wilt not hear, but shalt be drawn away, and worship other gods, and serve them; I denounce unto you this day, that ye shall surely perish, and that ye shall not prolong your days upon the land, whither thou passest over Jordan to go to possess it.*

I call heaven and earth to record this day against you, that I have set before you life and death, blessing and cursing: therefore choose life, that both thou and thy seed may live.

God did the same thing with the children of Israel that He had done with Adam: He gave them a choice. He even told them to choose life. He told Adam not to eat of the fruit of the tree of the knowledge of good and evil. He gave him a choice and warned him of the consequences.

Now, before you get it into your mind that God is the One Who sends evil and cursing, let me assure you He is not.

Job 34:10,11 says:

Therefore hearken unto me ye men of understanding: far be it from God, that he should do wickedness; and from the Almighty, that he should commit iniquity.

For the work of a man shall he render unto him, and cause every man to find according to his ways.

Each one of us will have according to what we do. We will reap what we sow by having what we say. God has laid down the law which is His Word. The choice is ours. The will of God revealed in His Word will show us how to operate the word system correctly.

4

"Poor Old Job"

Let's take a look at Job in light of the word system. He was a man blessed by God in every area of his life. Satan had tried to get to him, but could not — as long as Job gave him no place. In fact, in the first chapter of the Book of Job, Satan accused God of blessing Job.

In verse 8, God began bragging on Job, saying he was perfect, upright, God-fearing, and that he shunned evil.

But Satan declared, "It's only because You have blessed him. You have built a hedge about him. Without the blessing on his substance and his life, he would curse You to Your face."

Then God reminded Satan of the power he already had as a result of Adam's treason. He said, *Behold, all that he hath is in thy power; only upon himself put not forth thine hand* (v. 12).

God was not bargaining with Satan as some have thought. No! A thousand times, no! He was standing on His own Word, using His own system. God had given Adam authority in the earth; but Adam gave it to Satan. So God made a covenant between Noah, Abraham,

Moses, David, and so on, to establish a relationship of responsibility in the earth for mankind. God has done His part; now man has to do his.

Job had failed on his end of the covenant. In chapter 3, verse 25, Job said, *For the thing which I greatly feared is come upon me, and that which I was afraid of is come unto me.*

Evidently, Job was fearing calamity would come upon him. He had opened himself to the attack of Satan by allowing fear into his heart. (The devil smells fear like a dog smells meat!)

Fear in a man's heart produces fear in his words. People who are afraid talk fear. Job 1:5 tells us that Job offered sacrifices for fear that his sons had sinned and cursed God.

God stood firm on His Word concerning Job; it was Job who failed. God, in confrontation with Satan, only spoke good of him. He confessed that Job was perfect and upright and that there was none like him on the earth.

God was operating in faith; Job was not.

Job broke down the hedge God had placed around him by his words. Ecclesiastes 10:8 says, . . . *Whoso breaketh an hedge, a serpent shall bite him.* God can no longer be blamed for Job's suffering.

Finally, Job saw his dilemma and realized that it was his words which produced his captivity. The Lord answered Job out of the whirlwind and said, *Who is this that darkeneth counsel by words without knowledge?* (Job 38:2).

You see, all that Job had said was not completely true. Some of his statements about God, even though they were recorded in the Bible, were not necessarily true.

For example, in Job 1:21, he indeed said, *The Lord gave, and the Lord hath taken away,* but that statement was not true in regard to his situation. God did not take anything away; Satan did.

I saw an example of this on television in a John Wayne movie. John was a cattle rancher, driving his herd to the railhead in Kansas City and having to fight off rustlers. He shot a half-dozen rustlers along the way; and each time, he would dig a hole, bury them, and read this verse out of Job: "The Lord gave, and the Lord taketh away; blessed be the name of the Lord." I would laugh each time he said this because the Lord didn't kill those men, John did!

Then came the funniest, yet most truthful, line in the whole movie. After the last rustler had been buried, John's sidekick stood over the grave, scratching his head, and said, "You know, I can't figure out how John can shoot those rustlers full of holes, stick 'em in the ground, read over 'em and bring God in as a partner on the killing."

That may sound ridiculous, but there are millions of Christians who have done exactly the same thing. They have made God a partner in their failure when He was nowhere around.

God interrogated Job concerning his words. He said that Job had spoken wrongly of Him, that his words were void of knowledge. (Many Christians today have no personal knowledge of the Bible; they just listen to what somebody else says.)

God said to Job, *Gird up thy loins now like a man: I will demand of thee, and declare thou unto me* (Job 40:7). Then He begins to ask Job questions:

Shall he that contendeth with the Almighty instruct him? (Job 40:2).

Job answers, *I will lay mine hand upon my mouth* (v. 4). In other words, he was saying that he had spoken too much and now was going to hush.

Then God says something very important: *Wilt thou condemn me, that thou mayest be righteous* (justified)? (v.

8). I want you to realize the magnitude of this statement. Many times, Christians will blame or condemn God as the culprit in a situation so that the responsibility will not be on them.

I have heard Christians say it is not God's will for them to be prosperous or healthy, and they use that as an excuse for their dilemma. This is what Job did. God was trying to get him to see it.

It requires no faith whatsoever on your part when you put the monkey on God's back by saying, "Well, God must have wanted me to be sick for some mysterious reason." In other words, you can blame God all you want and justify yourself; or you can change your words and change your life.

Job finally saw his dilemma and repented:

Therefore have I uttered that I understood not; things too wonderful for me, which I knew not. Hear, I beseech thee, and I will speak: I will demand of thee, and declare thou unto me. I have heard of thee by the hearing of the ear: but now mine eye (spiritual eye) *seeth thee* (Job 42:3-5).

Some people have problems receiving the magnitude of Job's statement: *I will demand of thee, and declare thou unto me* (v. 4). Some scholars assume this portion of Scripture refers to God's words to Job in chapters 38 and 40. They say Job could not possibly be speaking this way to God. However, I want to remind you of some other times that men stood before God and spoke boldly to Him.

Take Abraham, for example. In Genesis 18 when he stood before God as an intercessor for Sodom and Gomorrah, he would not let go of God until he had interceded with Him for only ten righteous people in the city. He could have gone down to one. In fact, this is one of the most powerful conversations ever between God and man.

God said in verse 17, *Shall I hide from Abraham that thing which I do...?* He considered talking with Abraham before he made His move against the city.

In verse 31, Abraham said, *Behold now, I have taken upon me to speak unto the Lord.* He did this five times; but God did not mind, He desired it. This is what He wanted Job to do.

Moses was another man who spoke boldly to God in behalf of the children of Israel. Psalm 106:23 says that Moses *stood before him in the breach, to turn away his wrath.* Moses stood up and demanded of God.

In Ezekiel 22:30 God says, *I sought for a man among them, that should make up the hedge* (build up a wall), *and stand in the gap before me for the land, that I should not destroy it: but I found none.* God could not find a man who would stand before Him and demand of Him according to His Word.

God has always wanted a bold people who would rule. He wants a people who will use their authority in the earth and stand on His Word, demanding (asking) that righteousness prevail over iniquity.

In Malachi 3:10, God says, . . . *prove me now herewith, saith the Lord of hosts, if I will not open you the windows of heaven, and pour you out a blessing, that there shall not be room enough to receive it.* God is like the Marine Corps: He is looking for "a few good men."

When you see that God desires for His people to operate His system, it is not difficult to understand how He could spend nine months (and 42 chapters) getting Job to see the importance of the word system.

When he finally saw that his problem was his words, Job repented; and God blessed him with twice as much as he had before! The story of Job is not a story of suffering, but of redemption — and a perfect example of the word system.

5

Jesus, The Last Adam

In the Old Testament, the word system operated because of the covenant the people had with God. However, when Jesus fulfilled the Old Covenant, He reaffirmed the importance of the word system for the new creation.

Again, I want to use Genesis 3:1-6 as a basic text to show how Adam lost control of the word system through three principle temptations. Jesus reestablished the word system for the new creation believer by victoriously overcoming those same three temptations. God kept everything legal and in order. In all of this, we can see God's love for His creation.

Genesis 3:6 says, *When the woman saw that the tree was good for food, and that it was pleasant to the eyes, and a tree to be desired to make one wise, she took of the fruit thereof, and did eat, and gave also unto her husband with her; and he did eat.*

There are three factors in this temptation: the tree was "good for food" (lust of the flesh); it was "pleasant to the eyes" (lust of the eyes); it was "desired to make one wise" (pride of life).

This is how the word system was rendered inoperative for man. The power that God had bestowed on Adam — being made in the image and likeness of Himself — was to operate in this earth through words. The devil tempted them with the lust of the flesh, the lust of the eyes, and the pride of life; and Adam gave his authority to the devil.

But Jesus restored the system to the believer with His words. We see this in Luke 4:1-4. Jesus had just been baptized in the Jordan River:

And Jesus being full of the Holy Ghost returned from Jordan, and was led by the Spirit into the wilderness, being forty days tempted of the devil.

And in those days he did eat nothing: and when they were ended, he afterward hungered.

And the devil said unto him, If thou be the Son of God, command this stone that it be made bread.

And Jesus answered him, saying, It is written, That man shall not live by bread alone, but by every word of God.

Jesus spoke this from the 8th chapter of Deuteronomy, verse 3. The fruit of the tree of the knowledge of good and evil appealed to the lust of the flesh. It looked good for food.

The devil was not very smart. He used the same temptation on Jesus that he had used on Eve, but Jesus was ready for him. He had studied the Scriptures and knew the Word of God. By saying, *It is written . . . ,* Jesus reestablished in man the authority of the word system.

After the devil showed Him all the kingdoms of the earth, he said, *All this power will I give thee, and the glory of them: for that is delivered unto me; and to whomsoever I will I give it. If thou therefore wilt worship me, all shall be thine* (Luke 4:6,7).

Jesus again answered with the Word: *Get thee behind me, Satan: for it is written, Thou shalt worship the Lord thy God, and him only shalt thou serve.* (v.8; see also Deut. 6:5.) He again cut the devil with the sword — the Word of God.

Then the devil brought Jesus to Jerusalem, set Him on a pinnacle of the temple, and said, *If thou be the Son of God, cast thyself down from hence: For it is written, He shall give his angels charge over thee, to keep thee.* (vv. 9,10; see also Ps. 91:11.)

Jesus, unmoved and unhindered, comes back at him, saying, *It is said* (it is written), *Thou shalt not tempt the Lord thy God* (v.12; see Deut. 6:16).

Jesus took the Word of God from the Old Testament — the Old Covenant — and defeated the devil at his own game. He reestablished the word system for a new generation of men. He did not do this for Himself, but for you and me. Now we can speak the Word of God — uncompromised, full of power and faith — in Jesus' name, and see things happen just like they did when He spoke.

What happened after Jesus finished speaking God's words to the devil? It says the devil *departed from him* (v.13). He must have been angry. He had managed to keep the word system hidden, knowing that he was finished if man ever operated in the power God had originally delegated to Adam.

Satan's only weapon is deception. He used it on Adam and Eve and it worked: Man lost the ability to control his tongue and the word system began to operate against him. But God was not going to leave it that way. He sent Jesus as a man to legally reestablish the word system in the earth for us.

Jesus overcame the same three temptations that caused Adam to fail:

1. Lust of the flesh: Jesus said, *Man shall not live by bread alone, but by every word of God.*

2. Lust of the eyes: Jesus said, *Get thee behind me, Satan: for it is written, Thou shalt worship the Lord thy God.*

3. Pride of life: Jesus said, *Thou shalt not tempt the Lord thy God.*

Jesus used the word system in the face of temptation and triumphed over it. He was sinless, conquering death, hell, and the grave, regaining the keys for us. Colossians 2:15 says He spoiled principalities and powers, ruling and triumphing over them. He nailed to the cross the handwriting of ordinances that were contrary to us. (Col. 2:14.)

Why were those ordinances contrary to us? Because they were never intended for us. God did not want us to have them, to be crushed under the weight of them, so He sent Jesus to deliver us. We *were* delivered — and we still are!

Begin to speak the Word of God over your life. Get it down into your heart and speak it out your mouth. The word system was designed by God to produce, to create, to form, and to fashion. Put it to work in your life and you will reap its benefits: healing for your body, deliverance for your mind, prosperity for every part of your being.

6

Operating the Word System

Now, let's look into the operation of the word system. Jesus said:

The words that I speak unto you, they are spirit, and they are life (John 6:63).

I have not spoken of myself; but the Father which sent me, he gave me a commandment, what I should say, and what I should speak (John 12:49).

If a man love me, he will keep my words: . . . and we will come unto him, and make our abode with him . . . the word which ye hear is not mine, but the Father's which sent me (John 14:23,24).

In John 17:8, He prayed, *I have given unto them the words which thou gavest me; and they have received them, and have known surely that I came out from thee, and they have believed that thou didst send me.*

Jesus not only prayed to the Father and asked Him to give us His words, He even made a positive confession about the people who would receive the words: *. . . they have received them, and have known surely that I came out from thee.* He asked the Father to give us those words because He had reestablished the word system on the earth for the new creation.

We are to take the Word of God and operate it on the earth — not when we get to heaven, but right now. Jesus reestablished the word system for us so we could live like God intended us to live from the beginning — as a king, ruling over the creation.

God told Adam to subdue and take dominion over the earth. He was given total control and authority to rule and reign over everything he saw, whether above, below, or on the earth.

When Jesus reestablished the word system, man was to start where Adam had left off, to take total control over the systems on earth, to reign as kings and priests.

The value of operating the word system correctly is so that you can reign as a king and a priest in your life.

In the New Testament, we see the value of the word system in relationship to the name of Jesus:

Wherefore God also hath highly exalted him, and given him a name which is above every name:

That at the name of Jesus every knee should bow, of things in heaven, and things in earth, and things under the earth;

And that every tongue should confess that Jesus Christ is Lord, to the glory of God the Father (Phil. 2:9-11).

To say the name of Jesus, you have to speak words out your mouth. You get the ear of God when you speak the Word of God, in Jesus' name.

You have God's attention, but you also get the attention of everything else in the earth: *That at the name of Jesus every knee should bow, of things in heaven, and things in earth, and things under the earth.*

You can operate the word system for or against yourself.

If you take the words of God and use the name of Jesus, mixing it with faith, the system will work to your advantage for the purpose God created it: so you can live victoriously as a joint-heir with Jesus on this earth.

However, by speaking the words of the world, the word system will work against you as the words you speak carry death, sickness, disease, and failure.

The system is established. You can operate it any way you want. Proverbs 18:21 says, *Death and life are in the power of the tongue.*

Be aware of what you speak. Again, I point out Jesus' words in Matthew 12:34: *Out of the abundance of the heart the mouth speaketh.* Whatever you say and release faith in will come to pass.

I do not mean that if you say, "Oh, that tickled me to death," you will fall down dead, laughing. I am saying that if you continually build a life of negative words, based on fear, failure, sickness, and disease, you will produce that kind of climate around you.

If, on the other hand, you use the Word of God to produce a faith-filled atmosphere and climate of success, healing, deliverance, and prosperity, you will reap the benefits.

There is power in the tongue. The tongue is in the mouth, and the mouth speaks what the heart has in it. Death and life are within the power of your tongue. This is why Jesus said to be selective about what you hear.

Let's look at Matthew 12 and examine some other statements Jesus made. In verse 37, He said, *By thy words thou shalt be justified, and by thy words thou shalt be condemned.*

He preceded this statement by saying: *A good man out of the good treasure of the heart bringeth forth good things: and an evil man out of the evil treasure bringeth forth evil things. But I say unto you, That every idle word that men shall speak, they shall give account thereof in the day of judgment* (vv. 35,36).

We would be considered strange or weird by the people around us if we spoke nothing but the Word of God all the time. We would be considered peculiar by the world's standards, but not in God's eyes. The world does not realize the great power the spoken word holds over their lives.

Jesus said we will give an account on the day of judgment for every idle word we speak.

What are "idle words"? They are words that have no meaning, that carry no weight and have no knowledge in them. They are nonworking words. Remember how God told Job he had spoken words without knowledge? Idle words have absolutely no knowledge to them at all; they have nothing and do nothing.

Throughout the Proverbs, the Lord talks about fools who open their mouths wide. He says they will destroy themselves with their own words. Why? Because they are idle words with no meat in them. Jesus said to be careful of the idle words you speak.

Again, I refer to Jesus' words in Matthew, chapter 12: *By thy words thou shalt be justified and by thy words thou shalt be condemned* (v. 37). This principle goes back to the law of Genesis which says that everything produces after its own kind.

Why did Jesus say be careful of the words you speak? Because your words are containers that will justify or condemn you. Death and life are in the power of the tongue.

In Mark 11:23, Jesus said, in effect, that you can have what you say. If you speak death, you will have death. If you talk sickness and disease, you will have it. If you speak failure, you will fail.

There is a businessman who in the past put out some teaching that says a man becomes what he thinks about. When I was still in the business world, I heard him speak one day. I thought, That makes sense: A man is going to become what he thinks about because he is going to talk and do as he thinks.

When I got saved, I found out that his thought originated in Proverbs 23:7, *As he* (a man) *thinketh in his heart, so is he.*

When you really mean business about the word system, you find out that you cannot just talk anything. You cannot talk worldly trash and idle words; you must talk the Word of God. Everything produces after its own kind. When you speak the words of God, they will produce after their own kind because they are God's words.

Confession teaching is more than a "mouth trip." In Isaiah 55:11, God gives us a very important piece of information: *So shall my word be that goeth forth out of my mouth: it shall not return unto me void, but it shall accomplish that which I please, and it shall prosper in the thing whereto I sent it.* The Lord is saying that His Word must go forth before He is obligated to watch over it and perform it.

God has no responsibility over words that do not belong to Him. This is why He told the people of Israel in Deuteronomy 30:19: *I have set before you life and death, blessing and cursing: therefore choose life, that both thou and thy seed may live.*

By the words of your mouth, you choose life or death, blessing or cursing. What you say affects what you do; your saying and doing decide what you will have. You have control over these factors.

This is what people have misunderstood about God. They have thought God was taking control of everything. He is not. He has given you control to choose your own destiny by your words. You can either reject God or accept Him; He will not force you to serve Him. I do not mean to suggest that God has no control; but He has given us a part of that control here on earth.

This is what the word system is all about. You are operating the word system for or against yourself right now. Begin to speak the Word of God and the Word will obligate God on your behalf. I do not mean that He is bound; He enjoys being obligated to watch over His Word that He hears you speaking.

God told Joshua:

Only be thou strong and very courageous, that thou mayest observe to do according to all the law, which Moses my servant commanded thee: turn not from it to the right hand or to the left, that thou mayest prosper whithersoever thou goest.

This book of the law shall not depart out of thy mouth; but thou shalt meditate therein day and night, that thou mayest observe to do according to all that is written therein: for then thou shalt make thy way prosperous, and then thou shalt have good success.

Joshua 1:7,8

Now let's view this in the light of what we are teaching: operating the word system. Jesus said that the words you speak will justify or condemn you. He said out of the abundance of your heart, your mouth will speak.

God told Joshua that he could prosper and be successful. How? By meditating in the Word and being a doer of the Word.

Notice, the word "thou" (Old English for "you") is used eight times in these two verses. Many people are waiting for God to do everything for them, but He has already established His Word. He is waiting for *you* to act on what He has established.

You are to meditate in His Word, speak the Word with your mouth, and do all that is written in the Word. By doing this, you will cause yourself to prosper and have good success.

When Joshua meditated on the Book of the Law (God's Word at that time), it dropped down into his heart; he spoke it out his mouth and then observed to do all that was written therein. What happened? It caused him to be prosperous and successful.

Job experienced the same thing. (See Job, chapters 38, 40, 42.) God really did screen Job on his words. He told him that he had uttered words without knowledge. Job had contended with the Lord to instruct Him, but he could not because the words Job spoke had no knowledge in them. God said that Job needed to change his words.

In the last chapter of Job, he finally saw this. Job turned to God and said:

"Lord, I see it; I see it. My eyes didn't see it; my ears didn't hear it; but I see it now: things too wonderful for me which I knew not of. Listen, Lord. Hear me, I beseech Thee. I'm healed, I'm blessed, I'm worth it."

Some people say, "How dare Job talk to God like that!"

Well, that is exactly what God had been trying to get him to see for nine months. He wanted Job to see that his words were wrong. In fact, Bildad came to him one day and said, *How long wilt thou speak these things? and how long shall the words of thy mouth be like a strong wind?* (Job 8:2). When some people talk, it's like a wind blowing; their words are like hot air; there is nothing to them.

God can only perform over His words. Let me show you from Romans 10 how God performs over His words. This chapter deals with a person entering into the kingdom of God.

In verse 9, you confess with your mouth the Lord Jesus, believe in your heart that God raised Him from the dead, and you are saved, or born again. You enter into the things of God. But look at verses 6-8:

The righteousness which is of faith speaketh on this wise, Say not in thine heart, Who shall ascend into heaven? (that is, to bring Christ down from above:)

Or, Who shall descend into the deep? (that is, to bring up Christ again from the dead.)

But what saith it? The word is nigh thee, even in thy mouth, and in thy heart: that is, the word of faith, which we preach.

The word of faith is in your heart. If the Word is in your heart, it will come out your mouth. When you say it with your mouth, it will be heard by your ears and go down into your heart again. It is a complete cycle: up from your heart, out your mouth, heard by your ears, received into your heart, up from your heart, out your mouth, heard by your ears, received into your heart . . .

Verse 10 says, *For with the heart man believeth unto righteousness; and with the mouth confession is made unto salvation.* Here is the principle: With the heart man believes and with the mouth confession is made unto. This is in direct line with Matthew 12:34: *Out of the abundance of the heart the mouth speaketh.*

It is vitally important that you get the Word of God into your heart and speak it out your mouth. That will activate the Spirit of God to operate over His Word and cause what you say to come to pass.

When you operate the word system, it will produce fruit in your life. You will discover that words are more than just idle conversation and that you must speak God's words. You must get the Word of God down into your heart, so that your mouth will speak and produce the right kind of fruit.

Now you have the principle involved in producing fruit: The Word is sown in your heart; your heart believes it; the mouth speaks it; and it comes to pass.

Don't be like some Christians who have allowed their mouths to keep them from operating and enjoying God's best. Study God's Word and this book; then you will know how to operate in God's word system.

Happy Caldwell accepted Jesus Christ as his personal Savior at the Grand Ole Opry House in Nashville, Tennessee, after attending a new Gospel radio program on February 11, 1972.

After that night, Happy's life began to change. Recognizing the call of God on his life, he resigned his job in the wholesale liquor industry and began singing and preaching the Word of God.

Happy and his wife Jeanne pastor Agape Country Church in Little Rock, Arkansas. With their son Ronnie, they travel throughout the United States conducting crusades and teaching seminars. Happy also hosts a radio broadcast, *Agape Country,* which reaches several states.